First World War
and Army of Occupation
War Diary
France, Belgium and Germany

58 DIVISION
Divisional Troops
511 Field Company Royal Engineers
16 November 1915 - 27 February 1916

WO95/2996/5

The Naval & Military Press Ltd
www.nmarchive.com
Published in association with The National Archives

Published by

The Naval & Military Press Ltd

Unit 10 Ridgewood Industrial Park,
Uckfield, East Sussex,
TN22 5QE England
Tel: +44 (0) 1825 749494

www.naval-military-press.com
www.nmarchive.com

This diary has been reprinted in facsimile from the original. Any imperfections are inevitably reproduced and the quality may fall short of modern type and cartographic standards.

© Crown Copyright
Images reproduced by permission of The National Archives, London, England, 2015.

Contents

Document type	Place/Title	Date From	Date To
Heading	58th Division 511th Field Coy. R.F. Jan 1917-May 1919 1915 Nov-1916 Feb And 1917 Jan-1919 May		
Heading	WO95/2996/5		
War Diary	Esher	16/11/1915	16/11/1915
War Diary	Claydon	17/11/1915	27/02/1916

58TH DIVISION

511TH FIELD COY R.E.
JAN 1917-MAY 1919

1915 NOV — 1916 FEB
and
1917 JAN — 1919 MAY

WO 95/2996/5

Army Form C. 2118.

WAR DIARY
INTELLIGENCE SUMMARY
(Erase heading not required.)

Hour, Date, Place	Summary of Events and Information	Remarks and references to Appendices
ESHER. 16/11/15	**Movements** The Company relieved at ESHER at 7.50 A.M. Arrived CLAYDON 1.30 P.M.	
CLAYDON 17-30 /11/15	**Strength** Men 27 men transferred from 3/1st London Field Co. Present Strength of unit: 6 Officers 211 Rank and file Horses & mules 26 horses and 10 mules transferred Present Strength 52 horses 10 mules	6 horses left at ESHER suffering from ringworm. J. M. Hewlin Capt. R.E.(T.F) O.C. 1/5th London Field Company.

511 COY

Army Form C. 2118.

WAR DIARY
or
INTELLIGENCE SUMMARY.

1/5th LONDON FIELD Cº

(Erase heading not required.)

Hour, Date, Place	Summary of Events and Information	Remarks and references to Appendices
CLAYDON 1-1-1916	Strength Men :— 7 Officers & 228 men Horses & Mules :— 48 Horses & 15 Mules	5 men waiting transfer to R.E. (H.S.) Field Cº [stamp: 58th (LONDON) DIVISION 2 – JAN 1916 GENERAL STAFF] P.J. Rynard Major R.E.(T) O/C 1/5th London Field Cº

Army Form C. 2118

WAR DIARY
or
INTELLIGENCE SUMMARY

(Erase heading not required.)

1/5th LONDON FIELD Cʸ
CLAYDON

Place	Date	Hour	Summary of Events and Information	Remarks and references to Appendices
CLAYDON	Feb 1st 1916		Nil.	

L.S. Pyman
Major R.E (T)
OC 1/5th London Field Cº

Army Form C. 2118

WAR DIARY
or
INTELLIGENCE SUMMARY
(Erase heading not required.)

1/5th LONDON FIELD Coy
CLAYDON

Place	Date	Hour	Summary of Events and Information	Remarks and references to Appendices
CLAYDON	Feb 27th 1916		3 Officers & 139 NCO's & men left for a four weeks Course in Pontoon & Heavy Bridging at BRIGHTLINGSEA.	
	March 1st 1916			

J.J. Rynveke
Major R.E.(T)
O/C 1/5 London Field Cy

www.ingramcontent.com/pod-product-compliance
Lightning Source LLC
Chambersburg PA
CBHW081515160426
43193CB00014B/2693